A Kid's Guide to Drawing America ™

How to Draw
Virginia's
Sights and Symbols

Melody S. Mis

The Rosen Publishing Group's
PowerKids Press ™
New York

To my mother's family, the Heaveners, who are proud of their Virginian heritage

Published in 2002 by The Rosen Publishing Group, Inc.
29 East 21st Street, New York, NY 10010

First Edition

Editor: Jannell Khu
Book Design: Kim Sonsky
Layout Design: Colin Dizengoff

Illustration Credit: Emily Muschinske
Photo Credits: p. 7 © Phil Schermeister/CORBIS; p. 8 © Valentine Richmond History Center; p. 9 © Virginia Historical Society; pp. 12, 14 © One Mile Up, Incorporated; p. 16 © Robert Landau/CORBIS (tree), © Farrell Grehan/CORBIS (flower); p. 18 © Gary W. Carter/CORBIS; pp. 20, 22, 24 © Richard T. Nowitz/CORBIS; p. 26 © James P. Blair/CORBIS; p. 28 © Buddy Mays/CORBIS.

Mis, Melody S.
How to draw Virginia's sights and symbols /Melody S. Mis.
p. cm. — (A kid's guide to drawing America)
Includes index.
Summary: This book explains how to draw some of Virginia's sights and symbols, including the state seal, the official flower, and Mount Vernon.
  ISBN 0-8239-6103-6
1. Emblems, State—Virginia—Juvenile literature 2. Virginia—In art—Juvenile literature   3. Drawing—Technique—Juvenile literature   [1. Emblems, State—Virginia 2. Virginia   3. Drawing—Technique] I. Title II. Series
  743'.8'99755—dc21

Manufactured in the United States of America

CONTENTS

Let's Draw Virginia

Virginia is famous for its beautiful historic homes and buildings. Mount Vernon, located in northern Virginia, was home to first U.S. president George Washington for more than 45 years. Monticello, in Charlottesville, was the home of third U.S. president Thomas Jefferson. Both are magnificent estates. You can visit these homes and see some of Washington's and Jefferson's furniture, books, and other personal items that are displayed.

The Booker T. Washington National Monument, located in Hardy, honors the monument's namesake. Washington founded the Tuskegee Institute in Alabama. This institute was one of the nation's first schools of higher education for African Americans. Washington was born into slavery in Virginia but became a leader for African American slaves in the 1800s. In Staunton, you can visit the Frontier Culture Museum. This is a living-history museum that explores what life on the Virginia frontier was like between the 1600s and the 1800s. Richmond is the capital of Virginia. Richmond also served as the capital of the

Confederacy, during the Civil War. The Civil War was fought between the Southern states and the Union from 1861 to 1865. The White House of the Confederacy, in Richmond, has exhibits that show what Southern life was like during the Civil War. More than half of the Civil War battles were fought on Virginia's soil. Today many of these battlefield sites are open to tourists. This book will show you how to draw some of Virginia's sights and symbols. Directions are under each drawing. Each new step is shown in red. You will need the following supplies to draw Virginia's sights and symbols:

- A sketch pad
- An eraser
- A number 2 pencil
- A pencil sharpener

These are some of the shapes and drawing terms you need to know to draw Virginia's sights and symbols:

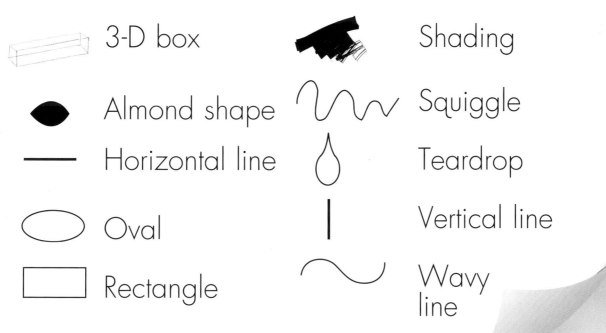

3-D box

Shading

Almond shape

Squiggle

Horizontal line

Teardrop

Oval

Vertical line

Rectangle

Wavy line

Old Dominion

Virginia's official nickname is Old Dominion because it was one of the dominions that belonged to King Charles II of England. In Norfolk, Virginia, there is even a university named after this nickname called Old Dominion University. Virginia has other nicknames. It is called the Mother of Presidents because eight U.S. presidents were born in Virginia. These include four of the first five U.S. presidents, George Washington, Thomas Jefferson, James Monroe, and James Madison. Presidents William Henry Harrison, John Tyler, Zachary Taylor, and Woodrow Wilson were the other presidents born in Virginia. Virginia is also called the Birthplace of the Nation, because English settlers founded Jamestown in 1607. Jamestown was the first English settlement in the New World. The New World is what Europeans first called America. Virginia was named for Queen Elizabeth I of England. She was called the Virgin Queen, because she never married.

This is the Washington and Old Dominion Trail that runs from Arlington to Purcellville, Virginia. Virginia is called the Mother of States because Illinois, Indiana, Kentucky, Michigan, Minnesota, Ohio, West Virginia, and Wisconsin were once part of the western territories claimed by Virginia.

Artist in Virginia

Edward Beyer

Edward Beyer (1820–1865) was born in Germany. He studied art at the Düsseldorf Academy before coming to America in 1848. Beyer settled in Pennsylvania, but he traveled to Virginia in 1854. He was so impressed with Virginia that he stayed in the state for more than two years. Beyer painted many Virginian landscapes while he was there. Beyer made lithographs of 40 of his Virginia landscapes. He published them in *The Album of Virginia*, which became his best-known work.

Lithographs are pictures produced by a printing process called lithography. To make a lithograph, a picture is drawn on a flat stone with a greasy crayon. Water is sponged over it. Ink is rolled over the drawing. The greasy crayon repels the water but attracts the ink. The ink sticks to the drawing but not the wet areas. When paper is pressed to the stone, it picks up the picture drawn with the greasy crayon.

Take a look at Beyer's painting. He painted the

landscape in 1855. Salem is located on the eastern side of the Appalachian Mountains, near Roanoke, Virginia. Beyer captured the beauty and peacefulness of a southern town nestled in a mountain valley. The painting is not only decorative, it has historical significance. Beyer's landscape preserves how a small town in Virginia looked six years before it was disrupted by the Civil War.

© Virginia Historical Society

Beyer's painting *Churches, Blacksmith Shop, and College: A View of Salem in 1855* measures 29 x 48 inches (74 cm x 122 cm). Beyer found the beauty of Virginia's landscapes ideal to paint.

Map of Virginia

Map of the Continental United States

Virginia's eastern region is called the Tidewater. The tides from the Atlantic Ocean flow into the region's rivers. The Tidewater is made up of three peninsulas that are formed by creeks and rivers that flow into the Chesapeake Bay and the Atlantic Ocean. The state's middle region is called the Piedmont. This region has rolling hills and fertile land covered with forests. The Mountain and Valley region is west of the Piedmont. Mt. Rogers is Virginia's highest point at 5,729 feet (1,746 m). The Blue Ridge and Appalachian Mountains are in this region. The Shenandoah Valley lies between these two mountain ranges. This region of Virginia provides some of the most beautiful scenery in America.

1

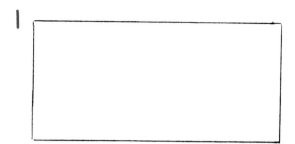

Begin with a rectangle.

2

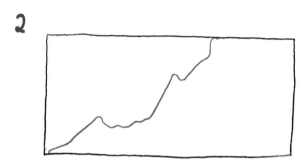

Next draw a ragged line to make the western border of Virginia.

3

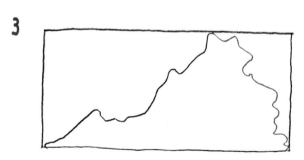

Add another ragged line to form the eastern border of the state.

4

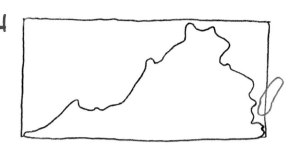

Add the island toward the lower right corner. This island is Delmarva.

5

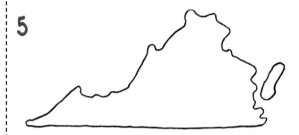

After you erase the rectangle guide, your drawing will look like the above.

〜〜〜	Chesapeake Bay
△	Colonial Williamsburg
☆	Richmond
〜	Shenandoah Valley
○	Virginia Beach

6

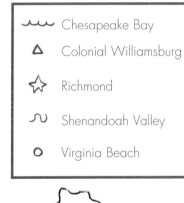

Let's add some of Virginia's key places:
a. Draw a wavy line for Chesapeake Bay.
b. Add a triangle for Colonial Williamsburg.
c. Draw a short squiggly line for the Shenandoah Valley.
d. Make a circle for Virginia Beach.
e. Draw a star for Richmond, the capital city.

The State Seal

The Virginia state seal was designed in 1776. Virtue, a Roman goddess, is in the middle of the seal. She is dressed like an Amazon. In ancient Greek mythology, Amazons were brave women warriors. As young girls, they were taught how to fight with bows and arrows. Virtue holds a spear in her right hand and a gold sword in her left hand. She stands over a dead male warrior whose crown has fallen off. He represents tyranny. Tyranny is a cruel form of government, in which the ruler uses his power to oppress the people. Underneath the male warrior is the state's motto, *Sic Semper Tyrannis*. This is Latin for "thus always to tyrants," which means that tyranny will always be defeated.

1

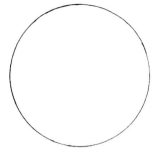

Start with a circle. Make sure the circle is large enough to fit in all the images you will draw.

2

Before you start to draw a stick figure of Virtue, study the figure. Notice that her left leg is straight and her right leg is bent. See how her arms are positioned. Draw one shape and one line at a time.

3

Next use the stick figure as a guide to fill in Virtue's upper body and arms.

4

Do the same to fill in Virtue's lower body. Next draw her dress. First draw her top and then add her skirt.

5

Draw Virtue's helmet. Next draw the stick figure that Virtue is standing on. Again, study the figure before you start.

6

Erase Virtue's extra lines. Use the stick figure as a guide to fill in the fallen man's body.

7

Draw details of the fallen man. Draw his crown. Next add Virtue's long spear and her sword.

8

Write "VIRGINIA" and "SIC SEMPER TYRANNIS." Finish by adding as much detail as possible. Shade your seal, and you're done! Nice work.

The State Flag

The Virginia state flag was adopted in 1861. The flag has a deep blue background. In the center of the flag is the Virginia state seal. The background of the state seal is white. Red flowers and green leaves form a border around the edge of the seal.

In 1954, Virginia adopted an official salute to the flag of Virginia. The salute goes like this:

I salute the flag of Virginia, with reverence and patriotic devotion to the 'Mother of States and Statesmen,' which it represents—the 'Old Dominion,' where liberty and independence were born.

1

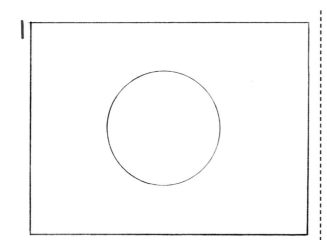

The first step is to draw a rectangle with a circle inside.

2

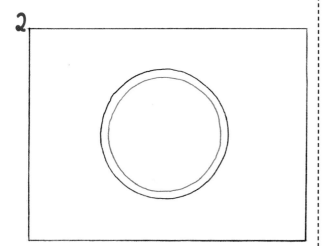

Add another circle inside the first circle.

3

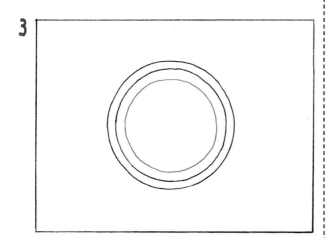

Add another circle inside the last circle you drew.

4

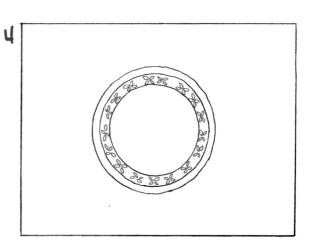

Draw a flowery border between the two inner circles. The flowers are made with groups of four almond-shaped leaves.

5

To draw the images inside the seal, refer to the previous chapter for instructions.

The Dogwood Tree and Flower

The dogwood became Virginia's state tree in 1956. It is a small tree and only grows up to 45 feet (14 m) high. The dogwood grows well in Virginia's moist soil. Dogwood trees grew on the grounds of President Thomas Jefferson's home in Charlottesville, Virginia, in the late 1700s. The wood of the dogwood tree is hard. It is used to make spools, on which thread is wound.

The flower of the dogwood tree became Virginia's state flower in 1918. Dogwood flowers have four leaves that look like petals. These leaves are called bracts. The flowers grow in the center of the bracts in tiny clusters. In the fall, the dogwood's leaves turn red, and the tree produces red berries.

1

Begin by drawing the trunk of the dogwood. Notice how it divides into four large branches.

2

Now draw the outline of the tree. Notice the fingerlike areas that poke out from all directions.

3

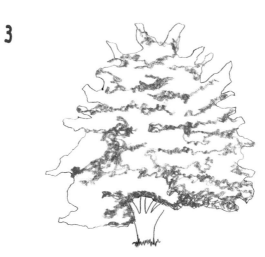

Tip your pencil on its side and start to shade the tree.

4

Continue to shade the tree. Make some areas darker than other areas. Fill in the trunk and the four main branches. You're done!

17

The Cardinal

Virginia adopted the cardinal as its state bird in 1950. The cardinal measures 8–9 inches (20–23 cm). The male cardinal has a bright red body. On his face, he has black markings that make it look like he wears a black mask! The female is a grayish brown with some red feathers on her wings and tail. Her coloring makes it easy for her to blend in with the surroundings to protect her babies. Cardinals live in Virginia's forests, fields, and gardens. They eat seeds, insects, spiders, and even snails. If an enemy approaches, cardinals can fly up to 25 miles per hour (40 km/h) to escape. Sometimes if a cardinal sees its reflection in a window, it thinks the reflection is another bird and attacks the window!

1

Begin with a diamond shape. This will be the guide that will help you draw the cardinal's head.

2

Next draw an egg shape for the body. The egg shape needs to overlap with the diamond shape.

3

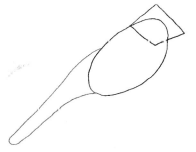

Draw the basic shape of the tail feathers. The shape looks like a finger.

4

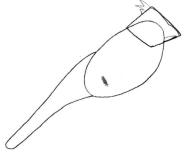

Use the diamond-shaped guide to fill in the outline of the cardinal's head. Notice the spiky feathers on its head. This is called a crest. Also notice the short, wide beak.

5

Erase extra lines. Next draw three lines for the wing and the tail feathers.

6

Add a circle for the eye. Draw a curved line to separate the beak from the head.

7

Draw a bigger curved line behind the first one you drew. Fill in the eye. Add more lines in the wing and tail areas. Start drawing the wood perch.

8

Shade the cardinal. Use the drawing above as a guide to shade some areas lightly and other areas heavily. Good job!

Luray Caverns

Luray Caverns, located in the Shenandoah Valley, are the largest caverns on the East Coast. Caves and caverns are formed by the movement of water and minerals through rock beneath the soil. Stalactites and stalagmites are formations found in caverns. They are formed by a blend of minerals and water that drips into the cavern. Stalactites look like huge, hanging icicles. Stalagmites grow upward from the ground. When the two meet, they form a column. One of the most interesting features of the Luray caverns is the Stalacpipe Organ. It hangs from the ceiling in the largest area of the caverns, the Cathedral. The "organ" produces music when the stalactites are tapped with electronically controlled rubber hammers!

1

Begin with a rectangle.

2

Use jagged lines to draw the stalactites that hang from the cavern's ceiling. Notice that the stalactites look like icicles.

3

Study the red lines shown above and copy them into your drawing.

4

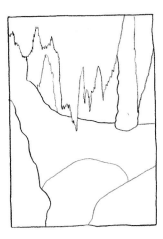

On the upper left side, add the triangular shape. Next draw two curved lines toward the bottom. You have drawn the basic shape of the cavern.

5

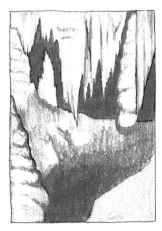

To finish you have to shade your drawing. Before you start to shade, look at the photograph of the cavern on the opposite page and at the drawing above. Notice where some areas are light and where other areas are dark.

Jamestown

In December 1606, led by Captain John Smith, three ships left England with 144 men. They left to find gold and to establish the first English colony in the New World. In 1607, the ships sailed into the mouth of a river and landed by an island. The men built a settlement there. The river was named the James River and the settlement Jamestown, for James I, king of England. Although gold was never found, colonist John Rolfe got rich by planting tobacco in Virginia's soil. Tobacco was the first crop to produce income for the settlers. Jamestown became Virginia's first capital in 1619. The settlers built a statehouse, but it burned down in 1698. The capital was moved to Williamsburg. Today you can visit the Jamestown Settlement, the living-history museum near Williamsburg.

1

First draw a straight horizontal line across your paper. This will be your guide as you draw the house. Next draw a rectangle. Notice the bottom of the rectangle slants downward toward the left.

2

For the roof, draw a vertical line that slants to the right and another one that slants to the left. Connect the two lines with a horizontal line.

3

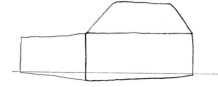

For the left side of the house, draw three lines. Notice how the bottom line slants downward to meet the bottom line of the rectangle you drew in step 1.

4

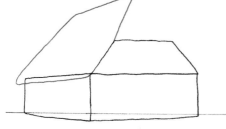

Next let's draw the left side of the roof. It is important to note the direction in which the lines slant. Draw the corners of the roof with soft, rounded lines.

5

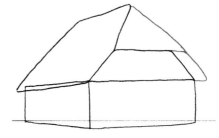

Draw three lines shown above in red to complete the middle and the right side of the roof.

6

Next add a door and two windows. Erase extra lines.

7

Add slanted, horizontal, and vertical lines to the house. Shade the door and the windows.

8

Shade the drawing. For the roof, press down on your pencil and draw a lot of small lines. You just drew a Jamestown Settlement house!

23

Colonial Williamsburg

Williamsburg became Virginia's second capital in 1699. Williamsburg was named for William III, king of England. When Richmond became Virginia's final capital in 1779, many Williamsburg residents closed their shops and moved away. The buildings started to decay. Then, in the mid-1920s, Dr. Goodwin of Williamsburg's Bruton Parish Church convinced millionaire John D. Rockefeller to rebuild Williamsburg.

Today Colonial Williamsburg is a famous living-history museum. You can experience what life was like in the eighteenth century. You meet villagers who wear eighteenth-century clothes, hear them speak about eighteenth-century ideas, and see how they make eighteenth-century household items.

1

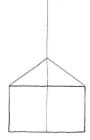

To draw the Governor's Palace in Colonial Williamsburg, first draw a rectangle.

2

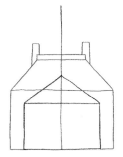

Lightly draw a vertical line in the center. This line will help you with the placement of the other shapes you'll draw. Add two slanted lines on top of the rectangle.

3

Add a larger rectangle outside the first one you drew. On top of the rectangle you just drew, draw the lines shown above. Next draw two thin, vertical rectangles and one thin, horizontal rectangle on top.

4

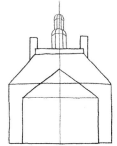

Draw a dome on top of the thin, horizontal rectangle. The dome has two sections, one on top of the other. Inside both sections of the dome, draw the lines shown in red.

5

After you erase extra lines, your drawing will look like the above. Next draw the windows.

6

Add details to the windows.

7

Draw the fancy door. Underneath the door, draw the stairway.

8

Add details and shading. Look at the photograph on the opposite page and at the drawing above and add as much detail as you'd like. Next shade your drawing, and you're done.

25

Mount Vernon

Mount Vernon was the home of President George Washington. Mount Vernon belonged to Lawrence, Washington's half brother. After Lawrence died, Washington inherited the estate in 1761. The estate included 2,000 acres (809 ha) and a Georgian-style mansion. Georgian architecture is simple and symmetrical in design. To be symmetrical means to be equally balanced. Washington enlarged the estate to 8,000 acres (3,237.5 ha) with five working farms that grew wheat, potatoes, and corn. Washington designed the impressive second-story porch that overlooks the Potomac River! After the White House, Mount Vernon is the most-visited historic home in America.

1

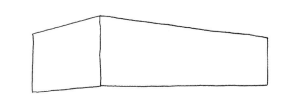

Draw two rectangles. Before you start, study the lines that make up the shapes. Notice that the horizontal lines slant either slightly up or slightly down.

2

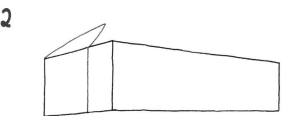

Draw a vertical line inside the left rectangle. On top of the same rectangle, draw two lines that slant to the right. These two lines need to come to a sharp point. This is the side roof.

3

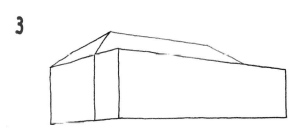

To finish the roof, draw the two lines shown above in red.

4

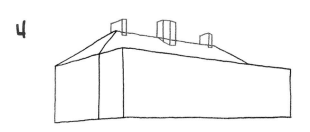

On top of the roof you just drew, draw a chimney on the left and on the right. Between the two chimneys, draw a rectangle. Notice that the bottom line slants downward. Inside this shape, add two vertical lines. This is the base of the tower.

5

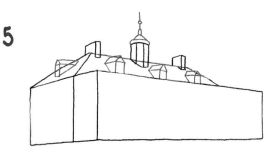

Finish the tower by adding the shapes shown in red. Add the dormers. Dormers are small windows that stick out of a roof. Study the dormers before you draw. You can practice on a scrap piece of paper before you draw.

6

Next add windows and the small entrance on the lower left. Notice that the entrance and the dormers have a similar shape.

7

Add eight columns.

8

Draw windows and doors.
Shade and you're done.

27

Virginia's Capitol

When Richmond became Virginia's final capital in 1779, a warehouse was used as the capitol building until a new statehouse was built. In 1785, Thomas Jefferson worked with a French architect to design the new statehouse. The statehouse was patterned after the Maison Carrée, a sixth-century Roman temple in France. One of America's treasures is in the rotunda of the capitol. It holds a life-size statue of George Washington. It was sculpted out of marble by French sculptor Jean-Antoine Houdon, one of the top sculptors of the eighteenth century. The cane Washington holds in his right hand represents the power of the people. The sword in Washington's left hand symbolizes military power.

1

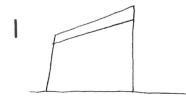

Draw a horizontal line across your paper. This line will help you with the placement of the other shapes you will draw. Now you are ready to add a slanted rectangle. Add a horizontal line at the top of the rectangle.

2

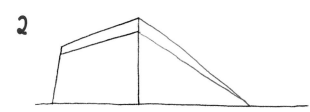

Draw two lines that slant downward toward the horizontal guideline that you drew in the previous step. This is the side of the building.

3

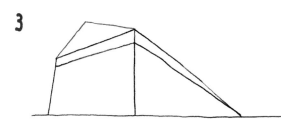

Draw two lines that slant to a point.

4

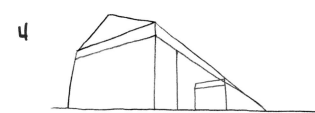

Look at the photograph on the opposite page. You will draw the small building that connects the two larger buildings. Let's start. Draw two vertical lines. Add two horizontal lines between the vertical lines. To the left of this small building you just drew, add a vertical line.

5

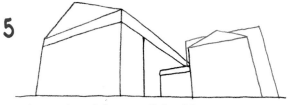

To the right of the small building you just drew, you will draw another building. Draw the lines shown in red. Notice that the horizontal lines slant upward and the vertical lines slant to the left.

6

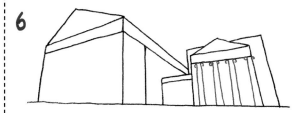

Next begin adding the columns. Each column is made with two lines and topped with a curl on each side.

7

Draw columns on the largest building. After you are done, there should be 11 columns total for all the buildings.

8

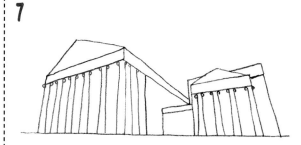

Next draw the windows. To finish your drawing add shading. Notice the way the shadow is deeper at the top of the building behind the columns. Nice work!

Virginia State Facts

Statehood	June 25, 1788, 10th state
Area	42,326 square miles (109,624 sq km)
Population	7,078,500
Capital	Richmond, population, 198,300
Most Populated City	Virginia Beach, population, 430,400
Industries	Transportation and electric equipment, textiles, food processing, printing, chemicals
Agriculture	Tobacco, vegetables, cattle, dairy products, hogs, soybeans, seafood
Dance	Square dance
Bird	Cardinal
Dog	American foxhound
Fish	Brook trout
Fossil	*Chesapecten jeffersonius* (scallop)
Insect	Tiger swallowtail butterfly
Shell	Oyster shell
Beverage	Milk
Boat	*Chesapeake Bay Deadrise*
Nickname	Old Dominion
Tree	Dogwood

Glossary

colony (KAH-luh-nee) A new place where people live, but where they still follow the rules of their old country's leaders.

descendants (dih-SEN-dents) People born of a certain family or group.

estates (eh-STAYTS) Large pieces of land, usually with large houses on them.

frontier (frun-TEER) The edge of a settled country, where the wilderness begins.

living-history museum (LIH-ving HIS-tor-ee myoo-ZEE-um) A museum that recreates the daily life of people from a historical past.

mythology (mih-THAH-luh-jee) Stories that people believed in during ancient times.

oppress (uh-PRES) To rule or control by cruel and unjust means.

peninsulas (peh-NIN-suh-luhz) Pieces of land that stick out into water from a larger body of land.

reflection (rih-FLEK-shun) The image of something seen on a shiny surface.

reverence (reh-VUH-rens) A feeling of deep love and respect.

rotunda (roh-TUN-dah) A round building, generally covered by a dome.

salute (sah-LOOT) To show formal respect by raising the right hand to the forehead.

significance (sig-NIH-fih-kents) Special or important meaning.

slavery (SLAY-vuh-ree) The system of one person "owning" another.

virgin (VER-jin) Not used or touched.

Index

Web Sites

To learn more about Virginia, check out these Web sites:
www.50states.com/virginia.htm
www.nauticus.org
www.mariner.org